PERFORMANCE FAVORITES

Volume 1

Band Arrangements Correlated with Essential Elements® 2000 Band Method Book 2

Keyboard Perc. Page	Timpani Page	Title	Composer/Arranger	Correlated with Essential Elements Book 2 Page
2	3	African Sketches	James Curnow	15
4	5	Barrier Reef	John Higgins	15
6	7	Do You Hear What I Hear	arr. Michael Sweeney	15
8	9	Regimental Honor	John Moss	15
10	11	Spinning Wheel	arr. Michael Sweeney	15
12	13	Streets of Madrid	John Moss	15
14	15	You're A Grand Old Flag	arr. Paul Lavender	15
16	18	British Masters Suite	arr. John Moss	32
20	21	Elves' Dance	arr. Paul Lavender	32
22	23	Firebird Suite – Finale	arr. John Moss	32
24	25	Gaelic Dances	John Moss	32
26	27	Irish Legends	James Curnow	32
28	* 29	On Broadway	arr. Michael Sweeney	32
30	31	Summon the Heroes	arr. Michael Sweeney	32
32	33	Two Celtic Folksongs	arr. Paul Lavender	32

* Includes a Percussion 3 part in place of Timpani

ISBN 1-423-45789-7

HAL•LEONARD®
CORPORATION

7777 W. BLUEMOUND RD. P.O. BOX 13819 MILWAUKEE, WI 53213

AFRICAN SKETCHES
(Based on African Folk Songs)

TIMPANI
(Bass Drum)

JAMES CURNOW (ASCAP)

BARRIER REEF
Overture For Band

KEYBOARD PERCUSSION
(Bells)

JOHN HIGGINS (ASCAP)

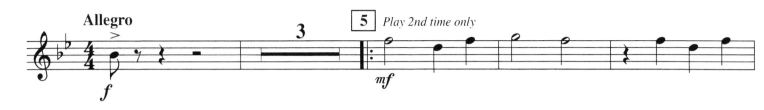

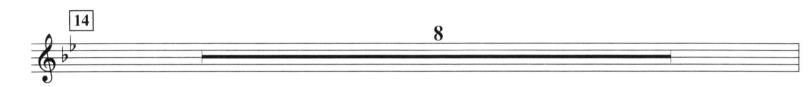

00860201

BARRIER REEF
Overture For Band

TIMPANI

JOHN HIGGINS (ASCAP)

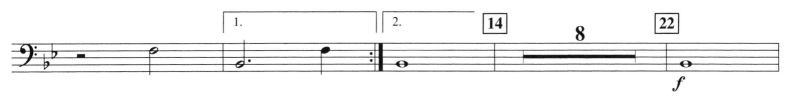

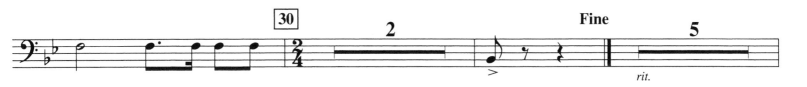

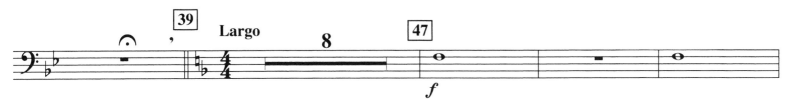

DO YOU HEAR WHAT I HEAR

**Words and Music by
NOEL REGNEY and GLORIA SHAYNE**
Arranged by MICHAEL SWEENEY

KEYBOARD PERCUSSION
Bells

DO YOU HEAR WHAT I HEAR

Words and Music by
NOEL REGNEY and GLORIA SHAYNE
Arranged by MICHAEL SWEENEY

TIMPANI

00860201

REGIMENTAL HONOR

KEYBOARD PERCUSSION
(Bells)

JOHN MOSS (ASCAP)

REGIMENTAL HONOR

JOHN MOSS (ASCAP)

TIMPANI

Recorded by BLOOD, SWEAT, & TEARS

SPINNING WHEEL

KEYBOARD PERCUSSION
(Xylophone, Bells)

**Words and Music by
DAVID CLAYTON THOMAS**
Arranged by MICHAEL SWEENEY

Recorded by **BLOOD, SWEAT, & TEARS**

SPINNING WHEEL

Words and Music by
DAVID CLAYTON THOMAS
Arranged by MICHAEL SWEENEY

TIMPANI

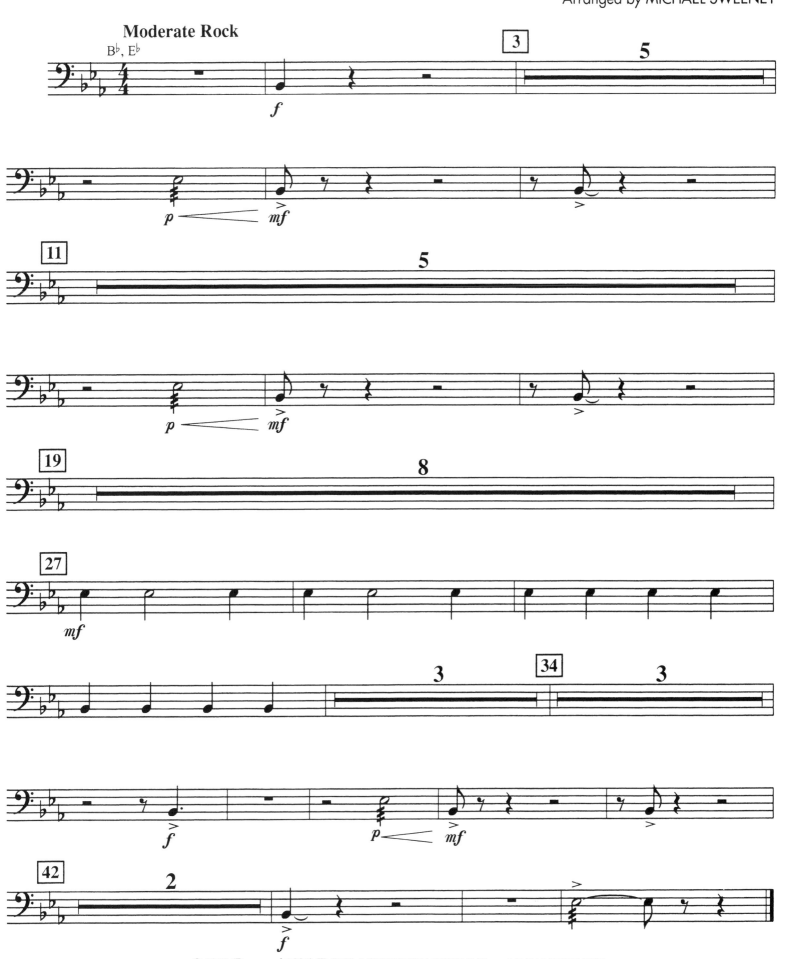

THE STREETS OF MADRID

KEYBOARD PERCUSSION
(Bells)

JOHN MOSS

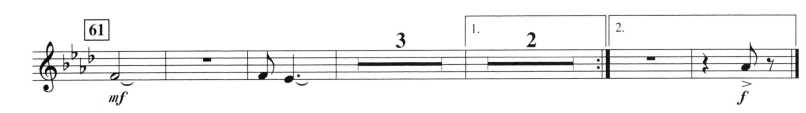

THE STREETS OF MADRID

TIMPANI

JOHN MOSS

YOU'RE A GRAND OLD FLAG

KEYBOARD PERCUSSION
Bells

Words and Music by GEORGE M. COHAN
Arranged by PAUL LAVENDER

YOU'RE A GRAND OLD FLAG

TIMPANI

Words and Music by GEORGE M. COHAN
Arranged by PAUL LAVENDER

Snappy March

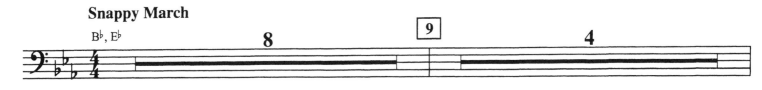

00860201

BRITISH MASTERS SUITE

KEYBOARD PERCUSSION
Chimes, Bells

Arranged by **JOHN MOSS**

I. Marching Song

GUSTAV HOLST

II. Nimrod (From "Enigma Variations")

EDWARD ELGAR

III. Sine Nomine

RALPH VAUGHAN WILLIAMS

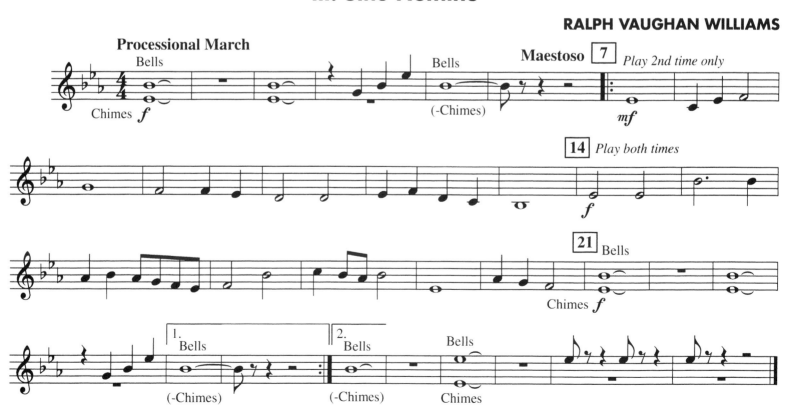

(This page left intentionally blank for a page turn.)

BRITISH MASTERS SUITE

TIMPANI

Arranged by JOHN MOSS

I. Marching Song

GUSTAV HOLST

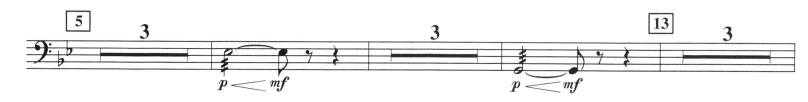

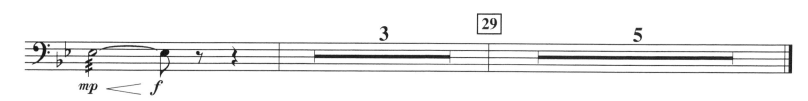

II. Nimrod (From "Enigma Variations")

EDWARD ELGAR

III. Sine Nomine

RALPH VAUGHAN WILLIAMS

ELVES' DANCE
(From The Nutcracker)

PETER I. TCHAIKOVSKY
Arranged by PAUL LAVENDER

KEYBOARD PERCUSSION
(Xylophone, Bells)

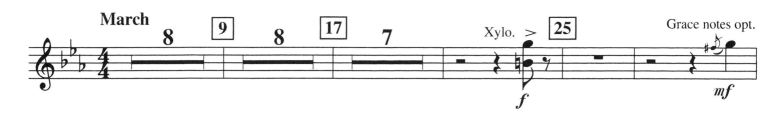

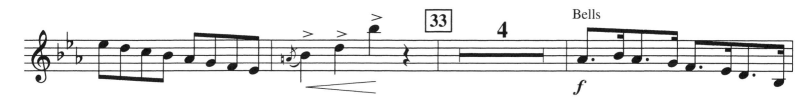

ELVES' DANCE
(From The Nutcracker)

PETER I. TCHAIKOVSKY
Arranged by PAUL LAVENDER

TIMPANI

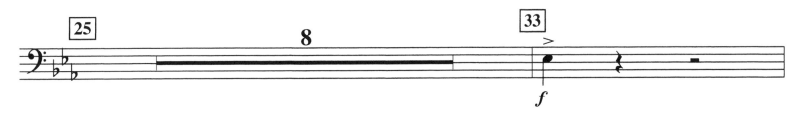

00860201

FIREBIRD SUITE – Finale

KEYBOARD PERCUSSION
(Bells)

IGOR STRAVINSKY
Arranged by JOHN MOSS

FIREBIRD SUITE – Finale

TIMPANI

IGOR STRAVINSKY
Arranged by JOHN MOSS

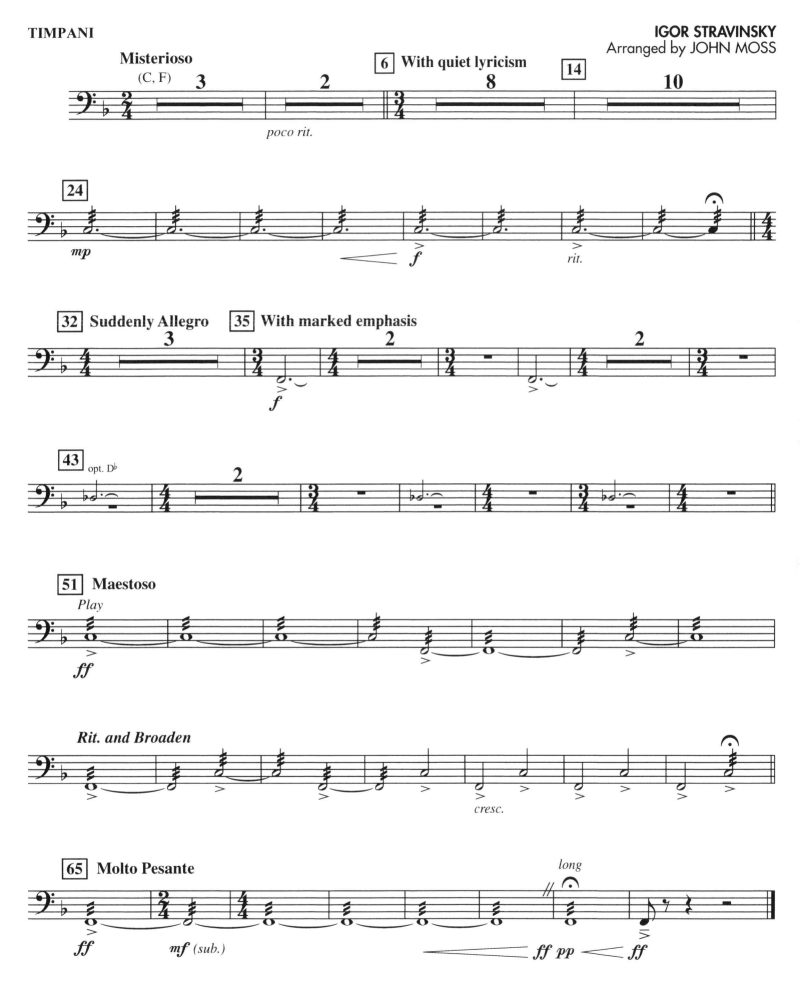

GAELIC DANCES

KEYBOARD PERCUSSION
(Bells)

Arranged by JOHN MOSS

GAELIC DANCES

TIMPANI

Arranged by JOHN MOSS

00860201

IRISH LEGENDS

KEYBOARD PERCUSSION
Bells

JAMES CURNOW (ASCAP)

Moderately fast

Bells-Plastic mallets

9 "Westering Home"

21

34

46 **Slower and with expression**
"In Dublin's Fair City"

54 **Somewhat faster**

65 **Fast and light**

67 "I'll Tell Me Ma"

75

Brass mallets

IRISH LEGENDS

TIMPANI

JAMES CURNOW (ASCAP)

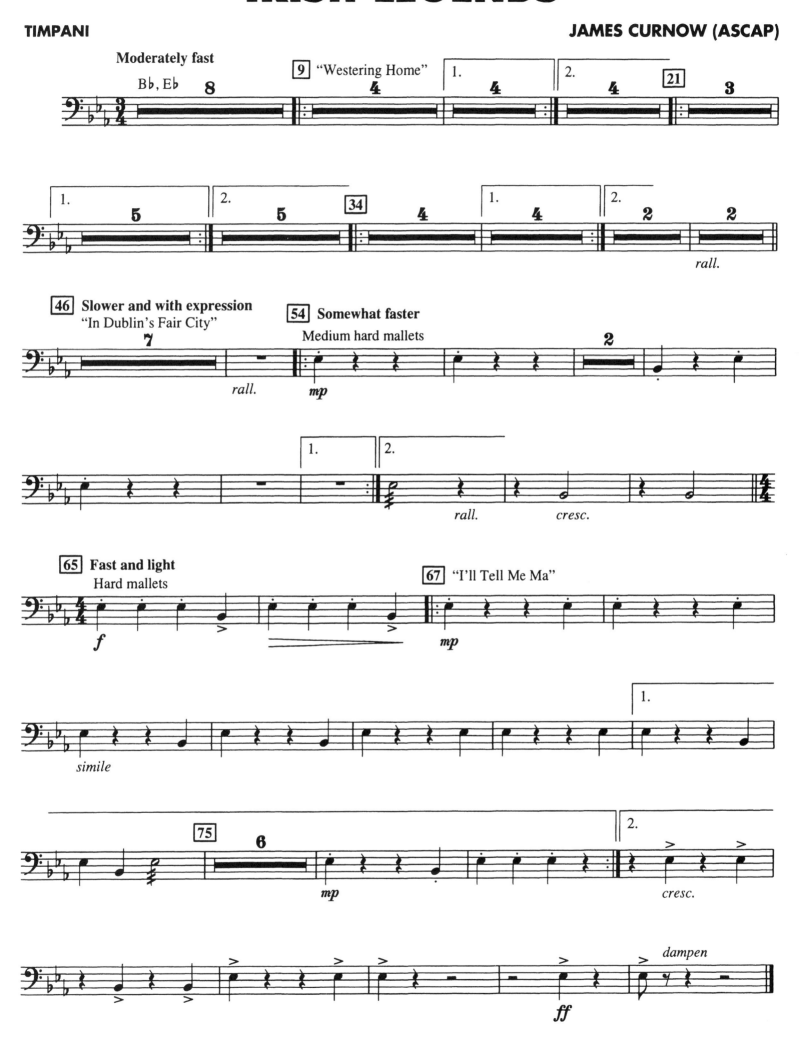

ON BROADWAY

KEYBOARD PERCUSSION
Xylophone, Bells

Words and Music by BARRY MANN, CYNTHIA WEIL,
MIKE STOLLER and JERRY LEIBER
Arranged by MICHAEL SWEENEY

ON BROADWAY

PERCUSSION 3
Bongos, Tambourine

Words and Music by BARRY MANN, CYNTHIA WEIL,
MIKE STOLLER and JERRY LEIBER
Arranged by MICHAEL SWEENEY

00860201

Written for the 100th Anniversary Celebration of the Modern Olympic Games

SUMMON THE HEROES

(For Tim Morrison)

KEYBOARD PERCUSSION
Xylo., Bells

By JOHN WILLIAMS
Arranged by MICHAEL SWEENEY

SUMMON THE HEROES

Written for the 100th Anniversary Celebration of the Modern Olympic Games

(For Tim Morrison)

By JOHN WILLIAMS
Arranged by MICHAEL SWEENEY

TIMPANI

00860201

TWO CELTIC FOLKSONGS
(The Maids of Mourne Shore • The Star of the County Down)

KEYBOARD PERCUSSION
Bells, Xylophone

Celtic Folksongs
Arranged by PAUL LAVENDER

TWO CELTIC FOLKSONGS

(The Maids of Mourne Shore • The Star of the County Down)

Celtic Folksongs
Arranged by PAUL LAVENDER

TIMPANI

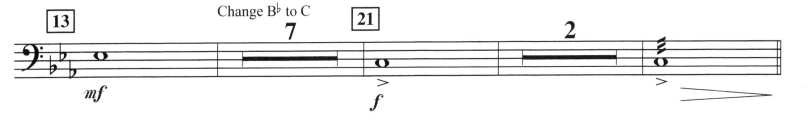